overheard
at
waitrose
II

quotes overheard in public

and transcribed by

nathan bragg

theresa vogrin

ISBN-13: 978-1-914117-04-6

*this book
is for
all waitrose customers
who brighten up our days
with their heartfelt
complaints
concerns
statements.*

*keep calm
and
carry on
shopping.*

contents

the
gossiping

i really don't understand
people who panic buy.
she has got toilet paper
and bags of dried pasta
piled high on her kitchen table.

well you never know
what's happening in people's lives
do you?

she may not have a larder.

the more expensive
the mineral water
the more thirst quenching it is.

fact.

when i die
i'm going to have
a bench put somewhere.

that's how much I like sitting down.

oh hello dear
how are you?
you'll never guess
why i'm here.

why are you here?

i'm here to buy
my grandmother
some laxatives.

i know my house
is hardly a palace
at the moment
with all the renovations.

but by god
hers is as rough as tits.

i'm broke.
like literally broke.
i've had to budget myself
down to only £200 a month
on eating out.

yah
it's really
that bad.

i'm pretty sure
male chickens
don't lay eggs.

                              they only find out
                              if a chicken is female
                              when an egg pops out.

rachel?
oh no
i haven't bothered with her
since i found
asda smart price cheese
in her fridge.

i'm just going to
peruse the plums.

if sainsbury and asda merge
resulting in store closures
how can they continue to keep
the riff raff out of waitrose?

only in waitrose
do people panic buy
potted basil.

and how is tristan getting on?

> he is imprisoned
> at sheffield uni.

oh only *sheffield*?
arabella is locked up
in *cambridge*.

it is so depressing.
you can't find a house
around here
for less than £1.5m.

well that's the difference.

i can go to tesco
in my gym clothes
but i have to change first
if i'm going to waitrose.

i want to go to france
because i really like
pain au chocolate.

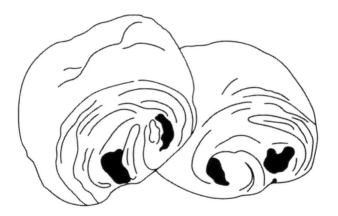

look at those poor cherubs
in the 10 rental properties
or less aisle.

it's not a salad
unless it has
quail eggs.

but i just want a cleaner
who understands
our cultural references.

it's not too much to ask.

ugh don't.
this is like the 13th christmas
i've been single.

it truly is depressing.

- girl aged 13

sometimes i feel poised
to get involved
with sourdough.

we just popped in
for a little hummus.

i do the big food shop
at harrods.

so tell me
about your new man.

ooh he is a *scientist*.

so exciting.

i know.
like an actual scientist.
he knows
so much *stuff*.

don't get me wrong
i care about the environment
and all that.

but no supermarket
is going to convince me
to cart around containers
like an old camel.

cecily
you absolutely must join
me and the girls
for an evening of
hummus and girly chatter.

she really is having
a hard time at the minute.

do you know
the other day i caught her
drinking tap water?

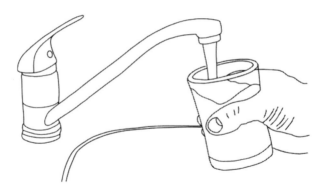

apparently
according to the grapevine
martha and her husband swing.

and not just once or twice either.

the worst thing
you can do
is put gin
into a tepid glass.

i can't believe
you used
the egg separator
to dish out olives.

i went to asda once
and the checkout assistant
didn't even know
what cambozola was.

rough as dogs.

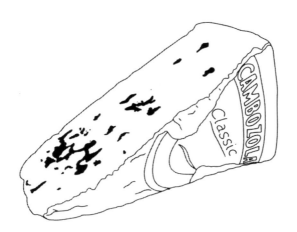

i wanted a botox cleanup
and she made me look
like joan bloody rivers.

when she was alive
of course.

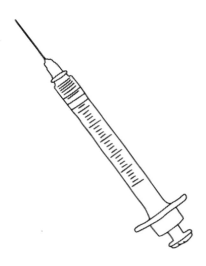

yes i shall be participating
in dry january.

i shall only be drinking
dry gin
dry white wine
dry cider
and dry sherry.

so unfair.
instead of skiing
they are taking us
to thailand for christmas.

i've already had
three hot holidays
this year.

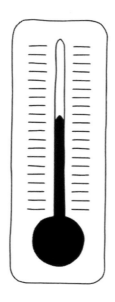

i was so stressed today
i bought
octopus carpaccio.

so i've decided
that the theme
for the new house
is going to be *forests*.

i'm on my last jar
of rose harrisa.

times are hard.

christmas eve
just before closing
waitrose reduced everything
to 50p.

it was awful.
reminiscent of when the peasants
stormed the winter palace
during the russian revolution.

i have given
myself
a croissant headache.

remember
when i bought spaghetti
instead of linguine?

mortifying.

well last night
was a disaster.
i only ended up
with basil
on the baby potatoes
instead of parsley.

luckily nobody noticed it.

people in this village
don't shop at tesco.

well the hubby
wants to get out of the eu
but all i wonder is
what if we are suddenly
not able to buy enough brie?

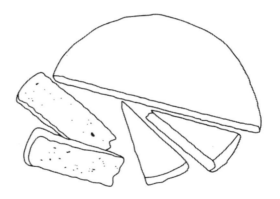

yes well they have
fresh sushi here
but let's be honest
we know that m&s
have a much better
selection of curries.

- *man on the phone*

i was so ill last night.
the drawback to living
in *such* a large house
is that the en-suite
is too far away
from ones sickbed.

ever since celia and the girls
got squirrels in the garden
i honestly haven't heard
the last of it from francesca.

we've had to promise her
a bloody pet squirrel
in return for good grades.

where on god's earth
do i get a squirrel from?

my god
the chilled aisle
is rather nippy.

good thing i brought
my mink coat today.

these steaks
have only been aged
a month.

probably in someone's dreadful pantry.

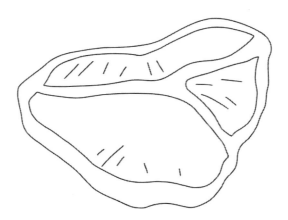

i know tesco is closer
but i will most certainly not
allow beatrice's pony to eat
everyday value straw.

i will strike you
with this cantaloup.

- two women arguing over the last duck on the shelf

gosh
you have to be
millionaires
to shop here.

just as well we are.

the
loving

hugo darling
whilst mummy parks the porsche
can you get daddy
a turbot and jerusalem artichoke sandwich?

make sure it's a meal deal.

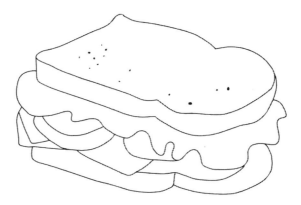

be careful.
i don't want you
bumping into any of those people
who only come in here
for the free coffee.

HAVE A COFFEE
ON US

remember
at this time of year
every instance of misbehaviour
could result in a reindeer
being taken outside and shot.

- mother to young son

i really can't be bothered.
shall we just buy
everything in here
and then throw away
what we don't want?

daddy
why can't alfie
eat real dog food?

because alfie is
a vegetarian
like the rest of us.

mum
with that scratch card
you could win
£40 000 a year
for life.

                                            yes
                        but you couldn't live
                                 on just that.

i told you the marmelade
wasn't down here.

no wonder daddy left you.

what fish would you like?

daddy
can we have
madagascan crevettes
please?

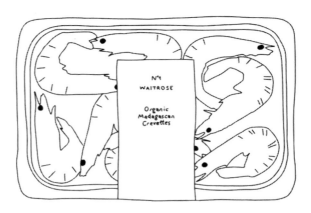

how do you expect us
to cope without basics
like olives?

we've got
twice the amount of focaccia
we need.

i do not know
what is going on here.

what would you like
darling?

to be heard.

- conversation between grandma and granddaughter

look
i'm very sorry
tarquin
but there won't be
any organic beetroot
for you this evening.

it's climate change
that's at the heart of this.

and a failing capitalist infrastructure
that requires a socialist revolution.

luciano behave.

children these days...
i blame the au pairs.

my child
you don't know
what *need* means
until you've *needed*
a glass of pimms
on a summer's afternoon.

go get the fucker
daddy.

it's foccaccia
claudia.

- little girl and dad

why do we have
dog food in the trolley?

                                    it's for the badgers.

oh you're brilliant.

quentin
find a cake
i can pass off
as homemade
for the village fête.

darling
what's the granola situation?

no jennie
you can't only serve olives
at your 10th birthday party.

now go and fetch a sirloin
for the dog.

so aidan
how are your chakras
doing today?

- *mother to toddler*

daddy, daddy
can i have this?

imogen.
life is *not*
a buying opportunity.

no raymond
you absolutely cannot
have a nespresso machine
in the playroom.

mummy
what's that next to
the dom perignon?

                                        that's cava.
                          you must never drink that.

well i'll have to
wipe my arse
with kitchen roll.

it's not ideal
but it's all we've got.

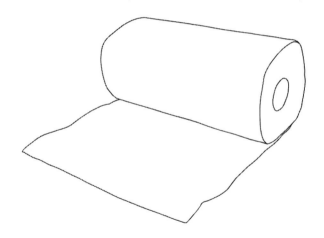

do we need
two or three cases of champagne
for christmas day?

don't be ridiculous.
your mother is coming.

of course we need another case.

no felix
that is not a stigmata.
that is a paper cut.

mummy
can i have a cigar
on my birthday?

no
mariana.
you are 16
and granny
will be there.

darling
come and look at this.

they have
plastic champagne flutes.

come along edgar.

please don't dawdle.

i told your father
we would be home
before the staff leave today.

- *mother to toddler*

oh no mother
those socks
won't do.

they are far
too cheap
at £7 a pair.

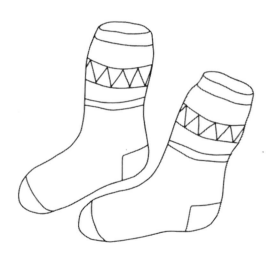

it's absolute carnage
in here.

no goji berries
no quails eggs
and no samphire.
all out of stock.

god knows
what i'm going to do tonight.

mummy
i wanted to invite fran
to my birthday party
but she told me
that her parents shop at tesco.

darling
i don't want to panic you
but they have
ran out of prosecco.

shall i try m&s instead?

they have
run out of ironing water.

will evian do?

darling
put that straight back.

purple sprouting broccoli
brings joshua out in hives.

no jessica
mummy is
not going to be seen
carrying pringles
to the car.

i told you
we shouldn't have come
to this till.

the woman in front of us
is paying using bronze coins.

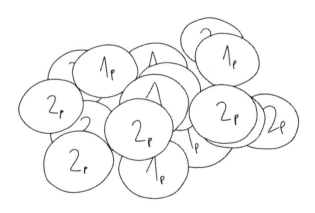

the
pestering

hi
have you got
a bag of farmers market english muffins
in lost property?

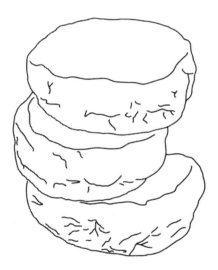

excuse me
what are these?

                              ready meals.

i thought they were
only for the poor
fat people.

i have to have
this many toilet rolls.

i have five bathrooms.

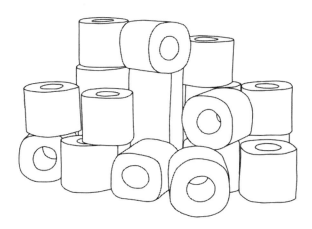

excuse me
were these partridges shot?

no madam
we managed to talk them
into surrendering.

jesus christ
why have you run out
of bloody pomegranate seeds?

madam
lower your voice.

this isn't asda.

the array of anchovies in here
makes going anywhere else
irrelevant.

wouldn't you agree?

- woman to staff member

there have been a lot of problems
since the sushi bar opened.

people are really upset
and up in arms
because the cheese bar
has been removed.

- cashier to customer

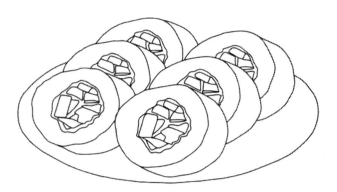

do you have
a sweetish wine?

        i don't think
       we've *ever* sold
        swedish wine.

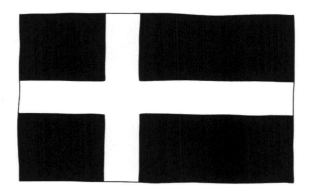

customers always ask
for polenta.
here it is.

what's that?

i don't know.
it looks like fufu
but it isn't fufu.

- staff member showing around a new staff member

excuse me
where might one find
the wasabi glazed popcorn?

is that salmon wild?

wild?
it was livid
when it was caught.

- man at fish counter

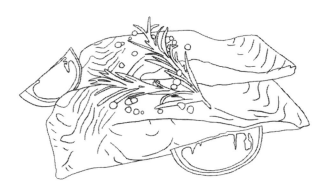

i can't eat cod.
that's a working class fish.

- *woman to staff member*

excuse me
do you stock
edible flowers?

m&s only stock
epoisse cheese in halves.

so i came
specifically for a full one
and now you're telling me
it's out of stock?

get me the manager.

which charity box
shall i put my green token in?

is there a box
for the retired butlers' home?

i wasn't being uncouth.

i simply said
you don't have
the correct kumquats
for the fruit salad.

- *woman to staff member*

i don't come to waitrose
to use the self-service.

if i wanted that
i would go to asda.

my housekeeper is ill today.
how do i use
this plebeian card reader?

what is a pin and chip?

i got so stressed out
with the garden
so my husband insisted
i went shopping at waitrose
to calm myself down.

- *woman to cashier*

if you enjoyed
overheard at waitrose II
please consider leaving
a review on amazon.

thank you.

other books published by *idiocratea*:

overheard at waitrose
overheard at whole foods
google search poetry
milk and brexit

about this book

overheard at waitrose II is a collection of the most iconic quotes overheard in waitrose stores and posted across social media platforms like twitter, facebook and instagram under the meme name *overheard in waitrose*.
this is the follow-up book of the bestseller *overheard at waitrose.*

idiocratea does not hold the copyright to the words, only to the illustrations and the presentation of the quotes. all credits go to the people submitting overheard conversations to the aforementioned social media platforms.

our only intention with this book is to make people laugh and brighten up their day.

about the contributors

nathan bragg

nathan bragg is a uk-based digital marketing specialist, entrepreneur, bestselling author and lover of memes.

theresa vogrin

theresa vogrin is an austrian bestselling writer, living in the uk. she published her debut poetry book *Bitter-Sweet* in july 2018.

check out her work on instagram at *@theresa_vogrin*

Printed in Poland
by Amazon Fulfillment
Poland Sp. z o.o., Wrocław